I Don't Want to Make My Bed!

Written by **Chris Yukevich**

Illustrated by **Sholto Walker**

Library of Congress Cataloging-in-Publication Data

Yukevich, Christine Cochrane Yukevich

I DON'T WANT TO MAKE MY BED! / Christine Cochrane Yukevich; illustrated by Sholto Walker

p. cm.

Summary: A little boy will propose almost anything so that he does not have to make his bed. Amazing what a little incentive will do!

ISBN:978-1518723988

[1. Chores – fiction 2. Young children—fiction 3. Stories in rhyme]

I. Walker, Sholto, ill. II. Title

For my cat, Lois,

who also loved a lumpy bed -c.c.y.

For children everywhere -s.w.

Please don't make me make my bed,

Pull up the sheets

And smooth the spread.

Why work so hard to make it right

When it will just get messed tonight?

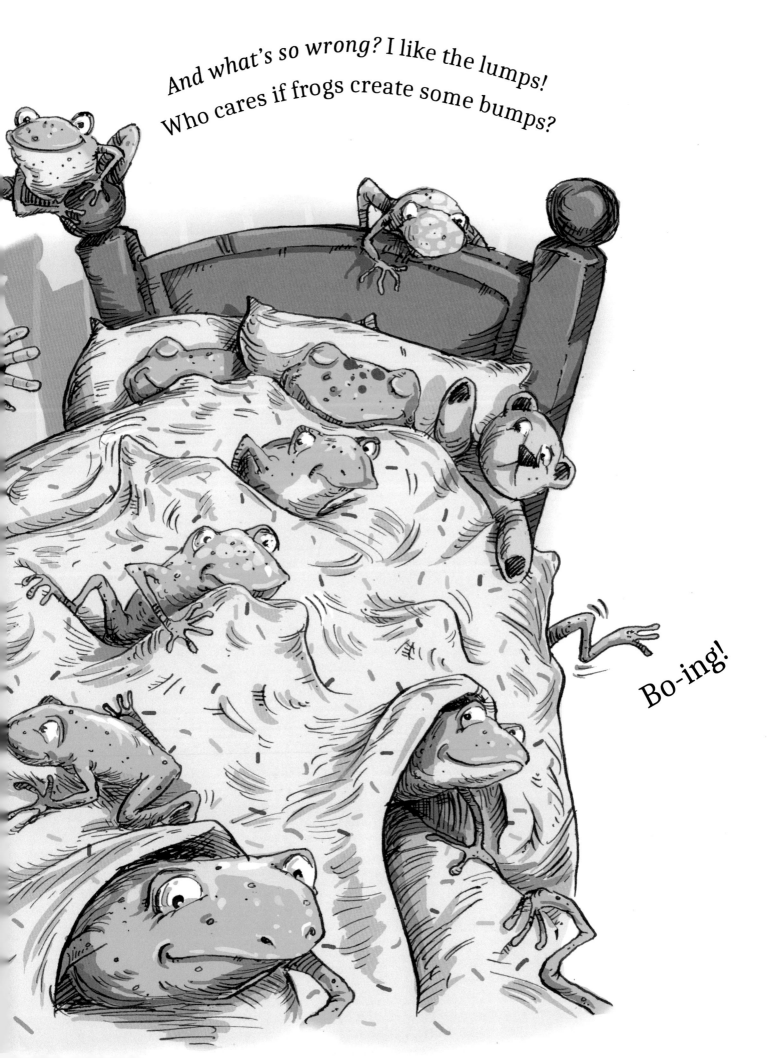

Do I HAVE to make my bed?

Now *that's* the job I truly dread.

How 'bout I take out all the trash?

I'll clean our dishes in a flash.

No need to ask, I'll wash the floor.

When that job's done, I'll *beg* for more.

Just count on me to feed our fish.

Whoops, I forgot *our* pets don't swish!

PUH-LEEEEASE don't make me make my bed.
This is what I'll do *instead*:
Each night I'll brush my teeth, I swear,
And once a year I'll wash my hair.

I'll stand up straight,

I will not slouch.

I won't shove food behind the couch,

I won't play bongos in the night,

I will not whine, I will not gripe,

I won't talk back. No! You will see

Grumble Soup will NOT be me.

And most of all, let me be clear,
When you say, "*Time for bed*" —

I'LL CHEER!

I DON'T WANT TO MAKE MY BED!

Would it matter if I said

I'll skip the puddles when it rains,

I won't jam sparklers

down

the

drain.

I'll keep my python in his pen,

I won't make crossed-eyes at Aunt Jen,

I won't swing from the chandelier,

I won't paint whipped cream on our mirrors,

No more wheelies in the dirt,

No more bronco rides on Burt,

No more spooks, no double dares,

No more skateboards on the stairs,

No more moonsaults from up high,

No more thumbs in Grandma's pies,

No more splats with water balls.

And it gets better, that's not all:
I will spell SASKATCHEWAN

Forwards …

backwards…

upside-down!

AND yes — *perhaps* — my toys I'll share,

All except my teddy bear.

Out there I will protect us all
From dragons and Neanderthals.

At night on flying pterosaurs
I'll SLAY the monsters near and far.

With brandished sword I'll...

Make my bed?

I'm *happy* to!

Now I'm through!

Made in the USA
Lexington, KY
26 May 2018